T0014362

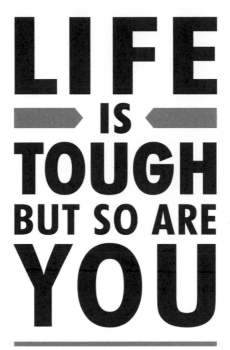

LIFE IS TOUGH BUT SO ARE YOU

Thoughtful Tips and Advice
for Developing Resilience
and Mental Strength

DEBBI MARCO

An Hachette UK Company
www.hachette.co.uk

Vie Books, an imprint of Summersdale Publishers Ltd
Part of Octopus Publishing Group Limited
Carmelite House
50 Victoria Embankment
LONDON
EC4Y 0DZ
UK

www.summersdale.com

Printed and bound in China

ISBN: 978-1-80007-155-1

Substantial discounts on bulk quantities of Summersdale books are available to corporations, professional associations and other organizations. For details contact general enquiries: telephone: +44 (0) 1243 771107 or email: enquiries@summersdale.com.

Disclaimer
The author and the publisher cannot accept responsibility for any misuse or misunderstanding of any information contained herein, or any loss, damage or injury, be it health, financial or otherwise, suffered by any individual or group acting upon or relying on information contained herein. None of the views or suggestions in this book is intended to replace medical opinion from a doctor who is familiar with your particular circumstances. If you have concerns about your health, please seek professional advice.

CONTENTS

Introduction   4

What is Resilience?   6

How to Boost Your Resilience   16

Self-Care   100

Seeking Help   144

Conclusion   156

Resources   158

INTRODUCTION

Ever wondered what the secret to happiness and success is? Surprisingly, it isn't luck or money or even non-stop hard work. The answer is a much-undervalued trait: resilience.

Don't worry, resilience isn't something you're born with; it's something you can learn and practise whatever your age or circumstances. While some people may seem as if they haven't experienced any setbacks or hardships in life, chances are they've had their fair share of struggles and disappointments. The difference is they have learned how to make the best of their situation, or they've simply been able to hide it. Now, with the help of this book and your own personal commitment to becoming a more resilient person, you can also become someone who knows how to bounce back from adversity. And not only will it make you feel happier, you'll also inspire others around you. By building your resilience you are much less likely to feel overwhelmed and stressed by life events. Instead you'll feel empowered, ready to adapt and prepared to move forward. So, what are you waiting for? Read on and start living your best life.

WHAT IS RESILIENCE?

Resilience is a wonderful thing, because the more you become aware of it and build it into your life, the easier it becomes to benefit from it. As you read the following pages, you'll begin to understand not only what resilience is, but how you can strengthen your own resilience and build it into your daily life. And it won't feel like a chore either: soon, being resilient will become second nature to you. As a result, life will feel much easier and more enjoyable.

RESILIENCE MEANS
YOU EXPERIENCE, YOU
FEEL, YOU FAIL, YOU
HURT. YOU FALL. BUT,
YOU KEEP GOING.

YASMIN MOGAHED

Be stronger than your strongest excuse

RESILIENCE IS A JOURNEY

If you've ever heard the phrase "when life gives you lemons, make lemonade" then you're already halfway to understanding resilience. It's the ability to keep going when life gets tough. But try not to make the mistake of thinking you're not being resilient if you are struggling with anxiety, stress or doubts. Resilience means you know how to keep going even when you're finding it hard, and you recognize that setbacks, loss and change are an inevitable part of life. Resilient people have learned how to tap into their strengths and their support systems in order to overcome adversity. But resilience isn't built in a day; it's something you can practise and work on to help you feel happier and mentally stronger as you journey through life.

A GEM CANNOT BE POLISHED WITHOUT FRICTION, NOR A MAN PERFECTED WITHOUT TRIALS.

Seneca

RESILIENCE IS A MUSCLE

Life isn't meant to be easy and it would be pretty boring if everything went to plan, with no need for a change in direction or creative thinking to get to the next level. But that's not to say it isn't exhausting, demotivating and downright depressing when things don't work out first time. But every time you overcome a difficulty or negotiate a down period of your life, you are growing and learning, and becoming a better, stronger person. It's a bit like when we exercise a muscle: we make micro-tears in the muscle, which grows back stronger. Think of life like a gym and your resilience as a muscle: the heavier your weights and struggles, the stronger you will become.

STRENGTH DOES
NOT COME FROM
WINNING. YOUR
STRUGGLES DEVELOP
YOUR STRENGTHS.

ARNOLD SCHWARZENEGGER

Resilience
is an art

Becoming resilient isn't like flicking an on/off switch. It takes time and effort, as we've established, but even then you have to keep applying the techniques you're about to learn on a daily basis. Resilient people have a mental palette of these techniques, and knowing which one will work best for any particular problem comes through trying them out on the canvas of real life and then looking closely at the results. This is the method that makes you resilient. You could see it as an almost scientific approach, but resilience is very much an art – and repeated training in this art will make you a master.

IF THE PLAN DOESN'T WORK, CHANGE THE PLAN – BUT NOT THE GOAL

HOW TO BOOST YOUR RESILIENCE

It would be lovely to simply read this book and immediately become more resilient, but unfortunately that's not going to be the case. The advice in the following pages will serve as your personal trainer, but it's up to you to get into the resilience gym and practise your new way of facing life's challenges. This chapter lays out some helpful suggestions to get you going and show you how you can stay calm and positive when life throws you a curveball. Not everything here might work for you, so try to adapt and find what works best in any particular situation.

MAKE A PLAN

Planning is a great response to tough times and a practical way of bringing good times into being. For any plan, organization is key, so think about how you can make it work for you. Perhaps you could make a timetable setting aside some time each day or week to work on tricky tasks or make progress towards your goals. Map out how you are going to get to a certain point in your life over the next 12 months. There are no rules when it comes to planning, but often having a deadline can help motivate you and keep you focused. Maybe you could wake up an hour earlier each day in order to work on your project or use that time to clear important tasks, leaving you free later.

TURN YOUR WOUNDS INTO WISDOM.

OPRAH WINFREY

TAKE A BREATH

It's so simple, but remember to breathe. Often, in times of stress and adversity, your breathing can get shallow and cause tightness in your chest. Take a few minutes each day just to check in with your breath. Breathe in through your nose for a count of five, hold for five and then release for five. Repeat this for five minutes a few times a day or whenever you have time. By concentrating on your breath, you will not only slow down your breathing to create a physical calmness, but your mind will also be soothed by the process of counting and by distracting yourself from negative thoughts.

Resilience is knowing that you are the only one that has the power and the responsibility to pick yourself up.

MARY HOLLOWAY

What's next?

Embracing change is one of the key elements to resilience as well as accepting that nothing stays the same. It's not easy to enjoy change if you are a person who is naturally nervous about things being different, but there are a few things you can do. Try not to dwell on the past and what has been, as you can't change any of this. Instead, see if you can ask yourself "what's next?" If you're actively looking forward and getting ready to face new

challenges, you'll be more prepared when they finally arrive. Keeping this in mind, try to be bold when you're moving forward. If you can make a big decisive stride into the future, it will take you a lot further than a tentative step. And you'll find that the more you face the future with determination and confidence, the easier it will become to embrace the changes that will inevitably come. This positive attitude will help you to make the most of each day and to achieve your goals.

MAKE CLEAR GOALS

If you're looking to build your resilience across all areas of life, take some time to set yourself some goals. Think about dividing them into short-term goals that you can achieve on a regular basis, such as creative projects or a commitment to exercise more. These should be easy to meet and enjoyable, so you can feel success and gratification on a regular basis. Also think about what long-term, complex life goals you have. These will take longer to achieve and will be harder work, but having a plan will keep you focused on the big picture. Keep your life goals achievable and try to break them down into smaller steps, to avoid getting overwhelmed. Long-term goals will help you to keep going even when circumstances threaten to knock you off track. Keep a diary or notes on what you've done to move towards your goals and the next steps you will take. Whenever you need some motivation, read back and see how far you've come. It's easy to lose track of the distance travelled if there is still a long way to go, but your progress is always worth celebrating.

Awaken your inner cheerleader

Most of us have an inner critic that whispers away to us when life isn't going well. But there's no need to let it bring you down. Remember that pretty much everyone has self-doubts and you are often harder on yourself than anyone else would be. When that nagging voice pipes up, instead of letting it bring you down, try some techniques to reduce its power. One is to mentally turn down the volume on all

the negative criticism, so you can barely hear it, and then turn up the volume on your inner cheerleader – the voice that tells you all the good things about yourself. Soon you'll get used to hearing your positive thoughts rather than the negative ones. Another technique is to thank your inner critic for its thoughts and then move on (you can do this out loud if you're on your own, or silently if you're in public). This way you're not ignoring your critic, but instead making the decision not to dwell on it. Any negative thinking will be short-lived, leaving you free to focus on the best way to move forward.

PAY ATTENTION TO YOUR EMOTIONS

When we're being emotional – either very cross or very angry – it is easy to dismiss our feelings as an overreaction, but it really pays to sit with your emotions for a while. Go somewhere private and quiet and try to make yourself calmer. Slow down your breathing by counting your breaths in and out, or perhaps try a visualization technique where you picture yourself on a desert island or somewhere else that helps you to feel more relaxed. Ask yourself some questions. Why did you react like that? Is there anything else upsetting you? Did it trigger something from your past? Try to figure out the answers and see if you can learn from what has happened. Your emotions are there to warn you or to remind you of something significant, so pay attention to them. Perhaps there is something else playing on your mind and causing you stress or anxiety. If you can work out what is really going on and learn to interpret your emotional reactions to things, you will be able to move forward so you can have a better reaction next time or deal with the underlying issues that are really bothering you.

Tell the truth

It's easy to believe the negatives, both the ones we tell ourselves and the ones that others say to us. Next time you have a negative thought, or someone says something unkind, examine the evidence. Can this so-called "fact" be true? If you've made a mistake at work, you might be tempted to quit or not put yourself forward for a promotion under the assumption that you're not good enough at your job. But instead of feeling defeated, sit down and consider the actual facts. List all the times you've done well at work or someone

has complimented you professionally. Of course, you may have made mistakes, but that doesn't mean you're a terrible person or bad at your job. Perhaps you need support from your line manager, or a mentor would really make a difference. This technique can be applied in any context, including friendships, relationships and just life in general. With the right attitude, you'll soon find that most situations can be turned into positive ones. It can be hard to do this on your own, so don't be afraid to ask a friend or loved one for help. And as with most things, the more you practise, the easier it will become.

Learn to fail well

It can be easy to view every time you fall short as evidence that you're not good enough or that you should give up. But try looking at it a different way. When you don't succeed first time, you're actually learning something. It could be that you make it the next time, but often it takes quite a few tries to succeed. And that's okay. If you never failed, you wouldn't grow as a person because you wouldn't be stretching yourself. Try making a list of everything you've learned each time something doesn't go quite right. View failure as an opportunity to build your resilience and keep doing better.

Don't give up – make the decision to start again

THE MOST CERTAIN WAY TO SUCCEED IS ALWAYS TO TRY JUST ONE MORE TIME.

Thomas Edison

IT DOESN'T MATTER HOW SLOW YOU GO, AS LONG AS YOU KEEP GOING

MORNING MANTRAS

When you wake up, set a positive mantra for the day ahead. A mantra can be a short phrase or sentence you repeat to yourself to encourage a positive mindset and support your well-being. Feel free to borrow one from this book or tailor one specifically to what's going on in your life today – perhaps you have a tricky work meeting that requires extra courage or you're feeling a bit wobbly when it comes to your friendships. Say it out loud a few times – perhaps even shout it if you can. Now keep it in mind all day and repeat it silently to yourself whenever you need a boost. You'll find the positive words will soothe your doubts.

Believe in yourself and you will be unstoppable

ASKING FOR SUPPORT

Asking for help is not a sign of weakness at all. Instead it shows that you're not willing to give up easily. If you're at work, speak to your line manager and explain what the problem is. Perhaps you have too many work projects all due to be completed at the same time or you haven't had the training you need to do one part of your job. If you can, when you present the problem also suggest a possible solution.

This shows that you've been thinking about your situation from all angles. If you just need a shoulder to cry on, try inviting a colleague out for coffee. You never know, they might be feeling the same way. If you're struggling at home, ask a family member or friend to help you. Maybe you need someone to do the laundry or cook dinner in the evenings because you haven't got the time or mental energy to do it. Or perhaps you just need a friend with a sympathetic ear to go for a walk with, so you have the time and space to process your problems. You'll find that reaching out and connecting to others is always a good idea and usually makes you feel better.

JOYFUL JOURNALING

Keeping a daily journal is more than just a way of recording events. It can help you identify any issues causing you concerns or anxiety, and it can help you track patterns and spot triggers that increase stress in your daily life. It's also a great way to learn positive self-talk (how you speak to yourself) and avoid negative thoughts and behaviour. Try not to put pressure on yourself to journal every day, but the more you make it a habit, the more you'll benefit from it. By emptying your thoughts onto a blank page you'll be able to get some perspective to help you negotiate any blocks that are stopping you from moving forward.

WE DON'T EVEN
KNOW HOW STRONG
WE ARE UNTIL WE
ARE FORCED TO
BRING THAT HIDDEN
STRENGTH FORWARD.

ISABEL ALLENDE

Enjoy the journey

When we're so focused on getting
everything right, it can be easy to forget to
ask whether it matters. Yes, getting to the
end of your to-do list can feel great, but
wouldn't going outside to play with your
kids or spending some quality time with
your partner or friend feel even better? It's
great to have goals and to achieve them,
but it is also important to keep things in
perspective. This doesn't mean you should
give up on your long-term ambitions, but
you should remember to take some time
to enjoy the journey along the way.

TURN CRITICISM INTO THE MOTIVATION YOU NEED TO KEEP GOING

Tackle the hurdles

Problem solving is a great way to get ahead in life, so it's good to think about sharpening up your skills. Regardless of whether you're facing an issue at work or difficulties within your friendship group, the road to the solution will be pretty similar. Try to remain objective and treat the challenge as if it is totally new. Create a list of potential obstacles that may prevent you from solving the problem;

this way, nothing will come as a surprise. View it as an opportunity rather than a big hassle, as taking the positive approach will make a big difference to your success. Be prepared to seek advice. Resilient people know that sometimes looking for help can be a good thing. And while you're busy solving problems, take stock and ask yourself how important it really is. If you look at the bigger picture of your life, how much of your time and energy does this problem really deserve? Try not to get wrapped up trying to fix small things when you would be better off letting go and focusing on something else.

GO OFF-PLAN SOMETIMES

Life doesn't always go to plan, so allow yourself to be open to the unexpected. If you're flexible, you might devise a unique solution or you might find yourself in situations you never imagined – and that can be a good thing. Being exposed to scenarios you didn't plan for and learning to solve problems that hit you from out of the blue will help tone your resilience muscles. And the next time the unexpected occurs, you'll be all the more ready to leap into action.

JUST BELIEVE IN YOURSELF. EVEN IF YOU DON'T, PRETEND THAT YOU DO AND, AT SOME POINT, YOU WILL.

VENUS WILLIAMS

FAKE IT TILL YOU MAKE IT

There's a lot to be said for faking it until you make it. This doesn't mean you need to live a life of lies. Instead, when you're feeling low or life events are threatening to stop you in your tracks, try to project the positive person you'd like to be. Dress, behave and speak to yourself and others with purpose and focus like you're a dynamic and determined winner. Soon the lines will blur and, before you know it, you'll be closer to the strong, confident person you are aiming to be.

Failure is simply a chance to revise your strategy

**If you really
look closely,
most overnight
successes took
a long time.**

STEVE JOBS

ROCKY TERRAIN MAKES YOU STRONGER

Check in
with yourself

Have you ever stopped to wonder if that
goal you're chasing is really for you? We
can get so wrapped up in focusing on
that promotion or being in a relationship,
we rarely stop to ask if it's really what we
want. It's a good idea to take time to check
that you're happy with where your life
is going. There's no shame in admitting
you've changed your mind or that different
things make you happy. Keeping an open
mind is often the secret to resilience as
it allows you to adjust your sails and
keep going, albeit in a fresh direction.

Asking for help is a sign of strength, not weakness

KEEP IT REAL

While we all want to be the best version of ourselves, chasing perfection in our personal lives or at work can be exhausting. Maybe it's time to stop setting such high targets and accept that life is full of wonderful imperfections. That is not to say you should give up on your dreams, but it might be time to apply a more realistic approach to your life goals. Why not break down your journey into easier stepping stones, rather than seeing it as a huge leap to the perfect end-goal? Take smaller "good enough for now" steps, which will help you keep your momentum.

I TRY NEVER TO USE THE WORD "FAILURE"… I CALL IT SOMETHING ELSE… "A STEPPING STONE TO SUCCESS".

Bear Grylls

HEAD INTO NATURE

Get outside and be inspired by nature. Take time to look closely at all the things around you. See how resourceful the birds are being by building their nests from any scraps they can find, while trees and plants bend towards the light, ensuring they get all the food they need. In all its richness and diversity, nature shows us that, by adapting to our environment, rather than fighting against it, we can learn to thrive.

IT'S AMAZING WHAT HAPPENS WHEN YOU WON'T GIVE UP

Make a
mood board

Making a mood board is a great way of reminding yourself what you're aiming for – and how great it will feel when you reach your goals. You can use your phone or computer, but you can also pin images representing your dreams and desires to a physical board. This will keep you motivated because seeing things laid out in front of you helps you to appreciate the bigger picture, while spending some time each day or week sitting with your board and tweaking different elements will keep your goals fresh in your mind. And the creation of a mood board can be pretty therapeutic and relaxing as well.

IF YOU GET TIRED,
LEARN TO REST,
NOT TO QUIT.

BANKSY

MIRROR, MIRROR

A daily pep talk can be just the thing when you need an extra bit of motivation to tackle a problem or get over a particular hump. Often, talking to your reflection in the mirror can help you get some distance between your inner critic and the truth. Although you might feel a bit silly doing it at first, make sure you've got some privacy and then give it a try. Look into your eyes first thing in the morning to set the tone for the day ahead, or reflect on how it went last thing at night.

The bamboo that bends is stronger than the oak that resists

MAKE A CHANGE

It can be tempting to think that resilience means you must keep going in the direction that you have set yourself, regardless of the obstacles that get in your way. But actually, agility, the ability to reflect and the willingness to change are all big factors in resilience. Knowing when to choose a different path or take a different approach to a problem are techniques that can be found in the resilient person's toolbox. While some people have learned how to do this alone, others may find that they need a team of friends and family around them to encourage them to keep finding their way. In time, you will discover what works best for you, but remember that changing your mind or your direction doesn't mean you have failed. Instead, it shows that you are a strong and intelligent person who can react with agility to the changing world. It might mean changing the path you're on, rethinking a relationship, planning a career change or returning to education. Remember, actively choosing to do something, rather than letting things simply happen to you, will help you feel more in control and convince you that you are moving forward towards a happier, more fulfilling life.

THERE ARE ENOUGH PEOPLE WHO WILL KNOCK YOU DOWN IN LIFE – MAKE SURE YOU'RE NOT ONE OF THEM

ALTHOUGH THE
WORLD IS FULL
OF SUFFERING,
IT IS FULL
ALSO OF THE
OVERCOMING
OF IT.

HELEN KELLER

BE YOUR OWN BEST FRIEND

You wouldn't give your friend a hard time for feeling low and struggling, so why are you doing it to yourself? See if you can get in the habit of treating yourself with compassion instead. Yes, life is hard and doesn't always go to plan. While it's okay to allow yourself to feel sad, also encourage yourself to get back up and start again. It might not be easy, so give yourself plenty of time, love and self-compassion, because you will get there in the end. And the more you do it, the easier it becomes, making self-kindness a habit you'll want to keep.

Boiling water softens a potato and hardens an egg: it's not about circumstances but what you're made of

Life is not a matter
of holding good
cards, but of playing
a poor hand well.

ANONYMOUS

Challenge yourself

It can be quite scary trying something new, but that is exactly the reason you should do it. Finding an exciting new hobby and committing to it will broaden your horizons in more ways than you realize. Not only will you be pushing yourself, you'll be using parts of your brain that you might not ordinarily tap into. Plus, you'll often be meeting people outside your usual social circles. It's a great way to make new friends and also show yourself that you can rise to a challenge. And small wins in one area of your life can often translate to bigger successes in other parts.

Lift weights

Sometimes, when you're carrying a heavy mental load, one of the best things you can do is pick up a physical weight. Weightlifting has been shown to boost moods and alleviate mild to moderate depression, leaving you able to think clearly and focus on your goals again. Experts believe that the mood-enhancing effect of weight training comes about because the proteins that muscles release when worked hard also support cognitive brain function – which includes memory, logic, reasoning and processing. This

means that when you head to the gym, you're not only strengthening your body, but your mind too. A quick session lifting some dumb-bells could give you a fresh perspective and help you to keep moving forward when times are tough. It will also boost your self-esteem as you watch yourself grow stronger and healthier. Remember to stay injury-free by starting light and building up to heavier weights. Ask a trainer for advice and tips or follow a programme on YouTube. You'll be surprised at how quickly you get stronger as long as you stick with it.

SWITCH IT UP

Sometimes, when life is testing your patience or your ability to weather its storms, you need to shake things up to inject the energy and freshness that will keep you motivated and invigorated. It could be anything from fitting in a run before you start your day to politely saying no to an unreasonable request at work. Things like finding the best time for exercise or speaking up for yourself will all have a knock-on effect on your confidence and well-being, helping you to face future struggles with greater assurance and assertiveness.

NO MATTER HOW MUCH FALLS ON US, WE KEEP PLOUGHING AHEAD. THAT'S THE ONLY WAY TO KEEP THE ROADS CLEAR.

Greg Kincaid

YOUR SPEED DOESN'T MATTER – FORWARD IS FORWARD

MAKE A LOVE LIST

We can often take the good parts of our life for granted – especially small everyday things. So instead of focusing on the negatives, start to note all the good in your life. And to really see these positives add up, try writing a gratitude journal or list. See if you can find up to ten things you feel grateful for each morning – this could be anything from a sunny day, hot coffee or upcoming dinner plans with a friend. Focusing on small wins and daily blessings means that, when life doesn't go to plan, you'll be able to see the bigger picture and realize you have a lot more beauty in your life than perhaps you first thought.

Get baking

It's not hard to make a simple cake, but you'd be surprised at how following a recipe and combining ingredients can help ease anxiety, and it also switches on different parts of your brain by keeping you focused and engaged. The soothing weighing and mixing of ingredients can take you away from any stresses and strains in your life. It doesn't even matter if you don't feel like eating cake, as you can give it away – who doesn't love receiving a home-baked cake? And if it doesn't work out first time, it's a great opportunity to practise your resilience and keep trying.

Don't wait for others to give you what you want – go and get it for yourself

I CAN BE CHANGED BY WHAT HAPPENS TO ME. BUT I REFUSE TO BE REDUCED BY IT.

MAYA ANGELOU

SHUT DOWN
YOUR SOCIALS

When life is weighing you down, it's easy to see social media as evidence you're not doing as well as other people. But when you're scrolling through Instagram or TikTok, remember what you're seeing is a tiny snapshot of someone's life. Unfollow any accounts that are making you feel bad or take a week off social media altogether. Use the time you would have spent online to figure out what's important to your happiness. Then introduce social media slowly back into your life and create boundaries. Try to only scroll for a certain amount of time each day. You'll find you have a lot more energy to put into your own life when you're not poring over someone else's.

FIND YOUR TRIBE

A great tactic for building resilience is to surround yourself with people who believe in you and cheer you on from the sidelines. This doesn't mean you should only be friends with people who agree with you and never challenge you; it means you should choose to spend time with people who have a positive influence on your life. For example, if you have someone who is forever putting you down, telling you that your ideas are no good and that you'll never make it, it can really bring you down and you could start to doubt yourself and your goals. But if you spend time with people who are positive, full of energy and bursting with creative ideas, they will soon start to inspire you. Limit the time you spend with toxic people or create boundaries when you see them. There's no harm in asking someone not to comment on your physical appearance or career choices as long as you are polite and firm. At the same time, maximize your contact with your own personal cheerleaders. Their kindness and positivity will help your resilience muscles relax, repair and be ready for the next challenge that comes your way.

Keep it clean

It can be really hard to stay calm and focused on your goals when you are surrounded by clutter and mess. It may feel like the ultimate in procrastination, but taking some time to clear up before you start a new project can actually help you get your thoughts in order. If you're struggling with a large amount of clutter, it's easy to feel overwhelmed, so start small. Choose a drawer, cupboard or surface to tidy. Once you've sorted that, move on to the next one. You'll soon find it quite cathartic to go through old things

and consider what is still useful in your life and what you no longer need. Before you start, prepare three bags or boxes to sort your items into: those you wish to keep, those destined for the bin, and those you want to donate. Try to be strict with yourself and avoid holding on to things you no longer need. Once you've succeeded in creating a more orderly space, you'll hopefully find that your mind feels clearer too. Also, as you start sorting through old things, you might find yourself inspired to start new projects or view a current one with a different perspective.

BE INSPIRED

It can be tough to keep going in the face of adversity, but it is possible. Look to some of life's heroes for inspiration. Whether it's Martine Wright, who lost both her legs in a terrorist attack and went on to compete in the 2012 Paralympics, or Nelson Mandela, who sacrificed so much for his beliefs. There are so many public faces and historical figures who have battled adversity and found a way through. Choose someone you can relate to and see if you can be inspired by their success – but remember, you can also learn from any mistakes they made along the way.

OUR GREATEST
GLORY IS NOT IN
NEVER FALLING,
BUT IN RISING
EVERY TIME
WE FALL.

NELSON MANDELA

DON'T LET YOUR FEARS DICTATE YOUR CHOICES

Learn to laugh

Laughter really is the best medicine and there's nothing like a good giggle to lift your spirits and help you get a new perspective on things. Chuckling can reduce stress and also help you cope when life isn't going as well as you'd like. So there's no better reason to settle down to watch your favourite sitcom or organize a night out with your funniest friend. Also, in almost any situation, no matter how grim, there is some humour to be found, which can be a valuable consolation in the moment, or it may make for an amusing anecdote in years to come.

SUPER STRETCHING

Whether you're a desk worker or spend too much time hunched over your phone, everyone can benefit from a good stretch, so don't feel as if you should limit stretching to after your workout. Stretching can not only improve your physical health and flexibility, but it can help you with relaxation. Remember to exhale as you stretch and never force it; let your body decide how far you can go. Hold your stretches for around 30 seconds and repeat two to three times for each muscle group. Stretching shouldn't cause pain, so stop straight away if anything starts to hurt.

No matter how dark it gets, the sun is still going to rise

If you're going through hell, keep going.

ANONYMOUS

STEP FORWARD

If you are feeling slightly overwhelmed by the tasks ahead of you, take one small action. You can choose to tackle something minor on your to-do list or try to deal with an issue that has been bothering you by taking a simple initial step. By dealing with problems head on, you will quickly prove to yourself that you are capable of taking charge and staying in control of situations. Even if you choose to just act on the small, easy-to-solve issues, these will all add up to helping you achieve your bigger goals.

Ditch your phone

Why not leave your phone at home when you're popping to the shop or heading out for a walk? We're so used to having a smartphone permanently in our hands that even on short journeys our heads are bowed over the small screen. When you're free of your phone, you will be able to look around you and see things you may never have noticed such as some colourful graffiti or a beautiful garden. Having a complete screen break will also help you feel more refreshed and focused when you get back. If you're concerned you might need your phone in an emergency, you can always take it with you and put it in flight mode at the bottom of your bag.

THE REAL TEST IS NOT WHETHER YOU AVOID FAILURE… IT'S WHETHER YOU LEARN FROM IT.

Barack Obama

BE A VOLUNTEER

Giving up your time to help someone else is one of the most positive things you can do. Sign up with an organization or charity, or just commit to helping a neighbour with their shopping once a week. By doing things for someone else, we boost our sense of well-being and belonging, and these feel-good emotions can have an impact on other parts of our lives. Not only will you be making a difference to others, but when you volunteer you are also connecting with people you might not otherwise meet. These connections will broaden your perspective and you never know how you might be inspired.

SAYING "I WILL TRY AGAIN TOMORROW" IS OFTEN THE BRAVEST THING YOU CAN DO

WRITE IT ALL OUT

You don't need to be a novelist to put pen to paper, but writing expressively can help you to get a different perspective and gain insight on the challenges you are facing. There are many ways to start writing, but one way is to get a blank piece of paper and pen (or use a computer if you are more comfortable with that), then set a timer for 20 minutes (you can increase this as you become more confident) and write down your deepest thoughts and feelings around a certain issue or problem you're struggling with. Try not to focus too much on your grammar or spelling or creating something that is entertaining or readable to others. This piece of writing is just for you to find out how you're feeling about something. Often, we bury our true thoughts and feelings so deeply that we can't consciously access them. But this activity can release them and bring them to the surface, allowing you to consider them with more insight than before. And don't be afraid to go deep, as you'll get greater clarity than if you stick to lighter, more superficial topics.

FACE YOUR FEARS

It's not easy to do things that scare us, but experience shows that when you face your fears, you can overcome them. By doing things you dislike, such as having an uncomfortable conversation or airing an unpopular opinion, you can build confidence and self-reliance. The more you face your fears, little by little at first, the better you become at doing so and the more you will believe in yourself. Not only will your life no longer be ruled by your fears, you'll also be more prepared for the future and more willing to take chances, because you'll have the confidence to do the things you find daunting.

IN THE END, SOME
OF YOUR GREATEST
PAINS BECOME YOUR
GREATEST STRENGTHS.

DREW BARRYMORE

SELF-CARE

Resilience is all about how well you can react when faced with adversity, but in order to do this, you need to look after your physical and mental health. Both are interconnected: by living a balanced and healthy lifestyle, you will be more physically and mentally robust. It's okay, you don't have to live in the gym, start running marathons and never enjoy a bar of chocolate ever again. But paying attention to your overall well-being will give you the energy, drive and positivity you need to win at the game of life.

Slow down

Introducing mindfulness to different aspects of your life can make a massive difference to your mental well-being. Mindfulness is the slowing down of your mind and focusing on one thing at a time in great detail. Focus on your breathing and try to bring your attention to the present moment. Do you notice any sounds, smells or tastes around you? How does your body feel? Can you feel any sensations? Once you get used to mindfulness you can apply it to daily activities such as going for a walk or eating your lunch. There are also plenty of apps for you to download to help you along.

When you're struggling to move forward, let go of the things that are weighing you down

TIME FOR A TREAT

When you're feeling low, it can sometimes feel as if you don't deserve nice things. But this is exactly the time that you should give yourself a treat. Perhaps it's a new book, a brightly coloured scarf or even a cup of coffee and slice of cake. Whatever it is, really enjoy it and tell yourself that you do deserve this. By reminding yourself you are worthy of nice things, it will help you see the value you have in the world. Start to think about the other things you're worthy of, such as healthy relationships or a rewarding job.

WHEN EVERYTHING
SEEMS TO BE GOING
AGAINST YOU,
REMEMBER THAT
THE AIRPLANE
TAKES OFF AGAINST
THE WIND, NOT
WITH IT.

HENRY FORD

Remember to relax

We can often find ourselves on the treadmill of life with no clear way to get off easily. Whether it is work, studying or taking care of family, putting yourself first often doesn't even make the list, let alone feature anywhere near the top. But burning out is no good to anyone, so try to give yourself a break. If you can take a whole day off, that's great. Plan a walk, visit an art gallery or even spend the day on the sofa with just you and Netflix.

However, a whole day to yourself can be hard to squeeze in if you have lots of responsibilities, so aim for two hours where you can prioritize your needs. Even sitting quietly with a cup of tea with your eyes closed for 10 minutes can be rejuvenating. Try to make this a regular thing. Each week, mark out time just for you where you can breathe deeply, collect your thoughts and regroup in peace. It's easy to say you don't have time, but once you have filled your own cup, it will be easier to re-enter life and help others fill theirs with new energy and focus.

RUN A BATH

A hot bath twice a week has been shown to boost your mood as much as exercise does, so make sure you book some bath time in your diary. It's the perfect solution if the weather isn't great and you don't fancy getting outside or you're just not up for a sweaty session at the gym. Simply add bubbles, candles and a good book, hop into the tub and linger as long as you like. Research suggests that a regular bath can restore the natural cycle of your body temperature, which changes throughout the day and night. If you're struggling with low moods, this temperature cycle might have been interrupted, and a regular bath is just the trick to help reset it. For an additional mood boost, try adding a few drops of essential oils such as jasmine and camomile, or if you're feeling a bit sluggish, try some cinnamon or bergamot oil to kick-start your energy levels. Lavender, meanwhile, will help ease feelings of anxiety and stress. Just remember to lock the door to ensure you're undisturbed for as long as you need.

Be kind

"Be kind" is so much more than a social-media hashtag. It really should be the mantra of your life. But we're not just talking about acts of kindness towards others, although of course they are important. We're talking about being kind to yourself. Self-kindness can take many different forms, whether it's allowing yourself to make mistakes, treating yourself to a day on the sofa watching TV, or ensuring you're eating a nutritious and healthy diet. Take a moment to think what you would give yourself if you were your best friend. Would

it be some kind words, a trip to the movies or a bowl of your favourite ice cream? Now see if you can do this for yourself, because whenever you practise self-kindness, you'll find you have more strength and capacity for life's little hiccups. Maybe choose this week to practise an act of self-kindness every day – plan it out if that helps you fit it all in, so you have no excuses to skip a day. Note how you feel before and after your experiment. It may seem indulgent, but it could soon have a positive effect on all areas of your life.

SUPERCHARGE YOUR SLEEP

Getting enough sleep is one of the most important things you can do for your mental and physical health, but many of us are still struggling to get enough quality shut-eye each night. Try to keep your sleep and wake times similar, so avoid a really late night or a long lie-in on weekends, although an hour either way is fine. Make sure you have a good sleep routine. Stop using your screen at least one hour before you sleep and try to keep all devices out of your bedroom so you're not tempted by a late-night scroll through Twitter. Keep your room as dark as possible – invest in blackout blinds if you need them. Treat yourself to a warm bath before bed and use calming essential oils such as lavender to promote sleep. There are also plenty of soothing pillow sprays available to buy or you can make your own. If you're still struggling to drift off, try listening to a sleep meditation app. It takes practice, but learning how to sleep better will improve every aspect of your life, so take some time to figure out what works for you.

PAY IT FORWARD

Have you ever had a stranger pay you a compliment or buy you a coffee for no reason? If you have then you'll know what a lift it gives you. And it works both ways. We tend to go about the world in a bubble, focused on how we can meet our own needs, but when you look outwards, to other people and their needs, the world can take on a whole new dynamic. Next time you're in a café, why not buy a coffee for the person behind you in the queue, or leave your favourite book on a park bench with a note on it for a stranger to find?

Hard times are sometimes blessings in disguise. We do have to suffer but in the end it makes us strong, better and wise.

ANURAG PRAKASH RAY

Time to meditate

The world is a noisy and busy place and it can be hard to find any calmness or stillness in order to collect your thoughts. So perhaps it's time to commit to a daily session of meditation – even five minutes a day is enough to have an impact. Find a quiet place and sit comfortably, making sure you're warm enough. Close your eyes lightly and focus on your breath, slowing your inhale and exhale to an even pace. Listen to the sounds around you – the

humming of traffic, the bird noises, people talking. Gradually allow the sounds to fade into the background and keep focusing on your breath. Whenever a thought appears in your mind, acknowledge it and let it go. When you are ready to finish your meditation, start to focus on the sounds around you again, allowing them to become louder. Finally, open your eyes. The more you practise, the easier it will become. You could try using a mantra to repeat when you meditate, or some essential oils to help relax you. You can also try guided meditation using an app such as Headspace if you would like some additional support.

YOU NEVER KNOW
HOW STRONG YOU
ARE, UNTIL BEING
STRONG IS YOUR
ONLY CHOICE.

Bob Marley

COURAGE ISN'T THE ABSENCE OF FEAR – IT'S FACING YOUR FEARS AND DOING IT ANYWAY

GET GARDENING

Gardening is a great way to increase your mood and your energy levels. The simple act of getting your hands dirty a few times a week can lead to increased well-being and lower stress levels. Even if you haven't got a garden to potter about in, you can achieve the same effect by growing plants on your windowsill or putting pots on your balcony. Or try to find someone with an allotment who needs a bit of help. Even getting out and about in nature will help distract you from any worries playing on your mind. If you've got a smaller space, think about growing herbs or microgreens to boost your diet at the same time. But if you have access to a bigger space, think about planting bright, fragrant flowers or grow some healthy fruit and vegetables for a double health boost. You'll find the acts of weeding, watering and simply plunging your hands into the soil will ease anxiety and may even give you a different perspective on problems that you're struggling to solve.

Eat the rainbow

Nourishing your body is just as important as looking after your mind, so make sure you keep an eye on the food you eat. This is not to suggest that you eat only salads and never treat yourself to your favourite snacks or ice cream (you definitely should treat yourself from time to time), but it is worth noting that while high-sugar, high-fat foods can make you feel good in the short term, in the long run they can leave you sluggish and tired. Instead, focus on eating a balanced diet at regular intervals

throughout the day. Eat a healthy breakfast with protein such as eggs or oats to keep you full for longer. Try to eat a rainbow of fruit and vegetables to ensure you get all the vitamins and minerals your body needs. Consider topping up with daily supplements such as iron and vitamin D, especially in winter. Keep a food diary for a couple of weeks to help you track what you are eating and what you need to eat more of. Often, we aren't eating enough fibre or omega-3 oils, all essential for good moods and a healthy brain. Make sure you drink plenty of water too, as dehydration can create feelings of tiredness and prevent clear thinking.

Write a self-love letter

Everyone loves receiving mail, but instead of waiting for someone else to write to you, put pen to paper and craft a compassionate letter to yourself. Take the time to acknowledge your strengths and forgive yourself for any weaknesses or mistakes. Think about where you'd like to be in your life in the coming years. Do you have any advice on how to get there? Try not to be critical; focus instead on being kind and gentle. By writing a letter you will create enough distance to be compassionate. You might be surprised to see more blessings and opportunities in your letter than you first expected.

You will get there, but only if you keep going

EASE OFF THE BOOZE

Whether you like a pint of beer, a cold glass of white wine or a fruity cocktail, drinking alcohol can seem a great way to unwind and release stress. However, if you drink too much, too regularly, alcohol can have a negative effect on your mood and physical health. But even if you just drink occasionally, you still have to deal with the potential consequences the following day, including a hangover and low mood. Try to have non-alcohol days each week and limit your alcohol intake on the other days. If you are worried about becoming reliant on alcohol, speak to your doctor.

OUR EXPERIENCES,
GOOD AND
BAD, MAKE US
WHO WE ARE.
BY OVERCOMING
DIFFICULTIES, WE
GAIN STRENGTH
AND MATURITY.

ANGELINA JOLIE

FIGHT YOUR WAY THROUGH

JOIN A TEAM

Whether you enjoy basketball, football or hockey, there are plenty of lessons in resilience in team sports – working together and keeping going when you're losing is just one of them. Being part of a team means stepping up to help your fellow players when they need you and vice versa. You'll notice how support from others really helps when achieving your goals. So, while a team sport is a great way to make new friends and keep fit, it will also strengthen your resilience muscles. By being part of a team on the pitch, you'll soon find you can transfer that courage and commitment to other parts of your life.

THE HUMAN
CAPACITY FOR
BURDEN IS LIKE
BAMBOO — FAR
MORE FLEXIBLE
THAN YOU'D
EVER BELIEVE AT
FIRST GLANCE.

JODI PICOULT

Don't compare yourself with others, only with the you from yesterday

PUPPY LOVE

Have you ever watched four-legged friends go about their day? Cats and dogs just merrily do as they please and are uninhibited about thoughts of failure and "what ifs". They really are an example to us all. But animals don't just show us how to live a carefree life – they're also great for decreasing anxiety and stress. Stroking a pet has been proven to reduce blood pressure and anxiety. Plus, if you own a dog (or can borrow one) the act of getting out and about to walk your four-legged friend can increase fitness and reduce your stress by adding structure to your day. You'll also meet fellow dog walkers, opening up a whole new community of people for you. In fact, studies have shown that pet owners are healthier and less stressed than those without a cuddly companion. One reason is that having a consistent routine keeps you and your pet balanced and calm. Having to feed, exercise and care for a pet can also help you to reflect on your own needs and how you can meet those as well. And it's not just cats and dogs that can help give you a boost: anything from gerbils to goldfish to corn snakes can have a positive influence on your life.

Get grounded

If things start to feel overwhelming or you're beginning to lose momentum and focus, take some time to ground yourself in nature. Choose your favourite outside space: it could be a sandy beach, a flowing river, a grassy field or simply a patch of earth. Take off your shoes and socks and stand for a moment in your chosen space. If it feels safe to do so, close your eyes. Wiggle your toes. Breathe deeply and concentrate on the textures beneath your feet and how this connects you to the

ground. Spread your weight, making sure the pressure is even from the ball of your foot to your heel. Feel the connection of the earth flow up into your body through your breath. Allow your thoughts to wander as you maintain your connection to the earth. If you prefer, you can use your hands and bury them in fresh soil, sand or shallow water. Whichever method you choose, it will help you feel relaxed and centred, with a fresh energy to face your life with calmness and purpose.

YOU ARE NOT DEFINED BY YOUR MISTAKES

Big up the positives

For many of us, criticisms and negative comments or thoughts are much easier to come by than compliments. Have you ever noticed that it's easier to believe a negative remark than a positive one? But how about you make an active decision to redress the balance? Set yourself a challenge and see if you can work to a five-to-one ratio. This means that for every negative thought you have about yourself or one of your goals, you think of five positive things. It might seem hard at first, but soon your outlook will become much sunnier.

BOOK IN A MASSAGE

When we're feeling overwhelmed and in need of self-care, a massage can be just the thing. Tense muscles can cause stress and drain our energy as it can be quite exhausting to carry that tension with us all the time. If you have the time and resources, book yourself in for a full-body massage or maybe even an Indian head massage. The type of massage doesn't really matter; it's just the opportunity to lie in a dark room with gentle music and have someone soothe your tense muscles. If you can't make it to a treatment room, you can always try a self-massage. Try to recreate a similarly peaceful environment with no harsh lights or loud sounds. Light candles and use essential oils with calming fragrances if you like. There are plenty of techniques explained online and you can always use tools such as a foam roller, which releases tension in muscles, or a tennis ball rolled between you and the floor or wall. Even rubbing your temples at the side of your head can make a difference to how you're feeling.

Know yourself

Self-knowledge is a wonderful and powerful thing. Once you truly see and understand all your strengths and vulnerabilities you'll be better able to navigate the tricky waters of life and whatever is thrown at you along the way. Sure, you might be knocked off course occasionally, but by understanding what you can handle and when you need to ask for support, you'll be better equipped to get yourself back on track.

Take some time out to conduct a full inventory of yourself. This means looking

at anything you're scared of and any areas where you could improve, and then writing them all down. Make sure you also take a good look at your strengths and all the positive parts of your personality. Chances are you'll be able to fill the "room for improvement" column fairly quickly, so reach out to friends, family and work colleagues and ask them what they see as your strengths. You could be surprised at what comes back. Hopefully, deep down, you know your true strengths and weaknesses, but seeing them in black and white can really help. Now you can be empowered by this knowledge.

A hero is an ordinary individual who finds the strength to persevere and endure in spite of overwhelming obstacles.

CHRISTOPHER REEVE

GET MOVING

Feeling mentally strong often comes from feeling physically fit. That's not to suggest you should work out in the gym until your muscles are bulging, unless that's what you love. But make sure you move your body every day. This can be a yoga or Pilates session, a regular walk or run, or perhaps a fun Zumba class. Not only will you get the benefit of feel-good endorphins, but you will become fitter and healthier. The extra oxygen being pumped round your body will also help your brain to think more clearly, which makes regular exercise a win on all levels.

SEEKING HELP

There is much truth in the maxim "a problem shared is a problem halved" and there are many people who can share the load. When you are struggling, asking for help can feel like a further failure, but reaching out for support rarely makes a problem worse. By talking to someone you trust, such as a family member, close friend, work colleague or even a professional, there's a good chance you will feel immediately better. This final chapter will help you weigh up who can help you the most and show you how to take the next step.

SHARE YOUR FEARS

It's hard to keep things all bottled up, and it's definitely not healthy. But it takes a really brave person to share their innermost fears and worries with a friend. So, muster your courage and choose someone who will have the time to listen to you. Trying to catch someone as they are rushing to school pick up or when they're late for a meeting will not give you the response you're looking for, so give plenty of notice to the person you intend to confide in. If you can, ensure the conversation happens face to face. There are lots of physical cues and reactions that can be lost in a phone call, but if you really can't be in the same room, try a Zoom call. There's a good chance your chosen friend will not have all the answers, but that's okay: you just need them to listen. Hopefully you'll feel better from talking to someone and knowing that they are there for you whenever you're struggling. So don't feel as though you have to soldier on alone – find someone to lean on.

Find a mentor

If you are feeling lost and overwhelmed, it's unlikely that someone else hasn't also felt this way at some point in their career. This is why many companies and businesses offer a mentorship programme. A mentor is someone slightly ahead of you in their career or specialism who can spend time with you and listen to your problems. They won't simply give you the answers to all your problems, but they will be able to guide you and support you as you

work out solutions for yourself. Having a mentor can be extremely empowering and it's a positive way to connect with people and benefit from their experiences – and sometimes their mistakes. They may also help you connect with their network, enabling you to make good contacts in your chosen path. Not all workplaces will facilitate mentoring, but you can always seek out a former manager or find helpful online communities related to your line of work.

IT IS NOT THE STRONGEST SPECIES THAT SURVIVE, NOR THE MOST INTELLIGENT, BUT THE ONES MOST RESPONSIVE TO CHANGE.

Charles Darwin

Let go of what's gone, be grateful for what remains and look forward to what is to come

FIND A THERAPIST

If you're really struggling, there are many paid therapists who specialize in all sorts of different therapies to help people. Speak to your doctor to see if they can recommend someone or, if you have a specific issue, there may be a charity which can help you connect with the right therapist for you. Whoever you choose, make sure they're reputable and connected to a professional organization.

It may take some time to find the right therapist, because like all relationships there needs to be a good rapport and level of trust. So don't be tempted to give up. If it doesn't feel right the first time you speak to someone, see if you can find someone else and start again. When you start to talk to a therapist, have a goal or outcome in mind. Most sessions last around 50 minutes, but you often spend the first one just checking the connection is right. There are lots of different options open to you, such as cognitive behavioural therapy, neurolinguistic programming and psychoanalysis. It all depends on your personal situation as to what will work best.

WHEN IT COMES TO SUCCESS, CONSISTENCY IS KEY

IT ISN'T WHERE
YOU CAME FROM,
IT'S WHERE YOU'RE
GOING THAT COUNTS.

ELLA FITZGERALD

CONCLUSION

This book has laid out many ways to create and nurture resilience in your everyday life. Through making small but powerful changes, you have the ability to adapt your mindset and your reaction to the difficulties you will face in life. You know now that mental toughness is not something you're born with – you can learn it along the way.

As you make your way through the world, try to practise the techniques you have learned throughout this book. If you make mistakes or find a particular method doesn't work for you, don't give up: take a break, learn from the experience and move on by trying something else. Remember to be flexible both in your goals and how you get there and, most importantly, be kind to yourself and others. Allow yourself to change and grow and keep on believing in yourself. You really are stronger than you know.

RESOURCES

For readers in the United Kingdom:
Anxiety UK: This charity provides information, support and understanding for those living with anxiety disorders. **anxietyuk.org.uk**

CALM: The Campaign Against Living Miserably (CALM) is leading a movement against male suicide. **thecalmzone.net**

Mind: This mental health charity offers support and advice to help empower anyone experiencing a mental health issue. **mind.org.uk**

Samaritans: A 24-hour, free, confidential helpline, to support you whatever you're going through. **Call 116 123; or email jo@samaritans. org (UK) or jo@samaritans.ie (Ireland)**

SANEline: A national, out-of-hours mental health helpline, offering specialist emotional support, guidance and information. **Call 0300 304 7000 (4.30p.m.–10.30p.m.); or email support@sane.org.uk**

For readers in the United States:
Anxiety & Depression Association of America: Education, training and research for anxiety, depression and related disorders. **adaa.org**

Freedom From Fear: A national non-profit mental health advocacy organization, helping to positively impact the lives of all those affected by anxiety, depression and related disorders. **freedomfromfear.org**

Mental Health America: promoting the overall mental health of all Americans. **mhanational.org**

Mental Health Foundation: A non-profit charitable organization specializing in mental health awareness, education, suicide prevention and addiction.
mentalhealthfoundation.org

National Suicide Prevention Line: A 24/7 free, confidential support service for those in distress, as well as crisis resources for loved ones. **suicidepreventionlifeline.org; or call 1-800-273-8255**

Have you enjoyed this book?
If so, why not write a review on your
favourite website?

If you're interested in finding out more
about our books, find us on Facebook at
Summersdale Publishers, on Twitter at
@Summersdale and on Instagram at
@summersdalebooks and get in touch.
We'd love to hear from you!

Thanks very much for buying this
Summersdale book.

www.summersdale.com